Through My Eyes

Poems by

Mike Abrahamian

ISBN 978-0-6151-5767-2

Published by Sivle Books
P.O. Box 41
Burbank, Ca 91503

Or visit us online
SivleBooks.com

4

I would like to thank everyone who believed in me and told me to keep pursuing my dream. Thank you from the bottom of my heart.

A special thanks to Corina Trifu for letting me use her beautiful drawing of Elvis.

Dedicated to everyone who has ever dreamed the impossible dream and made it come true.

Table of Contents

Introduction

I started writing poems over a year ago. This second book is my way of trying to create some positive feelings inside of people. So many things today are full of negative and depressing news or information. I hope that reading these poems gives you motivation and inspires you to remember that there are still good people in the world, you just need to give them a chance and help them out along the way. I myself was inspired by a kind and generous human being that I never had the opportunity to meet who was often misunderstood. He has inspired me to write through his music and beautiful soul. No matter who you admire or where you get your inspiration from, always try and share it with the people you love and those you might never meet. Always remember to try and stay positive because you never know who's reading your words.

Thank you Elvis for inspiring me to write.

Mike Abrahamian

Life Through My Eyes

I walk along the windy shore
wondering where she is...
As I feel the water splash across my
feet, I think to myself, she must be in
Heaven...
I feel abandoned and alone as I'm
walking by myself...
I say That's All Right Mama
because I know your not alone.

Searching through the woods for a
lost and scared dog...
I walked for miles in the dark night
hoping he'll be found...
Calling his name for hours with no
luck to be found...
I realized I was alone in the woods
walking in the cold Kentucky Rain,
searching for my best friend who had
lost his life just the other day.

I lay awake watching my little boy sleep...
Wondering how much he misses his momma...
I realize I'm a lonely man without my beautiful wife by my side...
My son awakes and sees my pillow wet with tears...
He looks into my eyes and tells me, Don't Cry Daddy, mommy is in Heaven with grandma and grandpa watching over us as we sleep.

Making my way through the
crowded city streets...
I look at all the trash and garbage
that lay just below my feet...
I wonder how anyone can ruin such
a beautiful street...
I hear gun shots and tires start to
screech...
I see a boy In the Ghetto run for his
life on these cold and lonesome
streets.

I made it back home from a war with no end...

I return to America the beautiful, my land of brave hearted men...

As soon as the plane reached the ground, I thanked the Lord and said amen...

I walked off the plane to see my beautiful wife waiting with our kids...

She asked if I had missed her, with a smile on her face...

I slowly kissed her lips and said "baby, you were Always On My Mind".

Watching the sun set just beyond the trees...
I realized she was dying and in need of some help...
Trying to bring her some water was too big of a task...
All I Needed Was The Rain to save her from the heat...
I looked up to the sky and prayed for some rain...
I slowly walked away and felt the heat go away.

After I left the restaurant and took
the short walk home...
I watched a lonely woman Crying In
The Rain...
I walked over to ask her if she was
in need of any help...
She looked up with tears falling
gently from her face...
She explained her heart was broken
and didn't know where to go...
Blue eyes Crying In The Rain, all
from being alone.

Walking into my newly bought house I felt like a King...
My wife was as happy as a clam to finally have a home...
I looked over at her and said Baby Lets Play House...
She smiled and started making plans for the newly bought home...
We settled in and gave the house a soul.

Seeing her hair blowin' in the wind
so gently and smooth...
I wondered where she came from as I
watched her beauty from afar...
She was beautiful and sweet, an
angel on earth...
I only wanted to meet her but never
had the chance...
I can only imagine why God made
her and put her on this earth.

*When I was young I waited for the
days to pass and for the weekend to
come...*
*I wanted to be free and out of school
to run around and have fun...*
*I couldn't wait to get older and have
my own car...*
*Now that I'm an adult, I want to be
young and running around in the
school yard...*
It's Funny How Time Slips Away.

Helping someone in need is a great feeling...
No matter what you give them or how much the amount...
Spread a little love and share with your fellow man...
From a dime in your pocket, or dollar in your wallet...
Give anything you can, to brighten someone's day.

Although we have different belief's
about Heaven and God…
We should respect each other's
wishes and make peace with all…
My vision of Heaven may be
different from yours…
We all have dreams of what lies
ahead…
Nobody should tell you that what
you believe isn't true.

Close your eyes and make a wish...
Find someone you love and give them
a kiss...
Give them a hug from time to time...
Let them know that you're happy,
that they're in your life.

They go to a foreign land and protect
us from evil...
We watch them leave our grasp, as
they head into battle...
We miss them and love them and
pray that the war will end fast...
They're freedom fighters who serve
Uncle Sam.

American fighters for all man kind...
Run into battle to save the dying...
Men and woman who fight as one...
Young and old, hero's they're all.

Fighting for their lives, in a foreign
land...
They are brave hearted souls, that
march into hell...
They protect each other along the
way, like brothers and sisters...
When they come home from that
foreign land...
Thank them and honor them, for
risking their lives.

*As you see a falling star, make a
wish from your heart...
Tell no one of this wish if you want
it to come true...
Wish for something that you want
because wishes really do come true.*

As I made my way down the
highway, on a dark and stormy
night…
I remembered all the good times and
fun that we had…
I was lost in the world without my
beautiful wife…
I drove for miles not knowing where
to go…
I saw a woman wearing a long
white dress, waiting for a ride…
I pulled over and gave her a lift…
She turned to me and said there's no
need to cry…
Your beautiful wife's been with you
the whole time you've been
driving…
As I looked to my right, this woman
in white was gone from my sight.

Running through the woods I feel
someone following me...
I run and run not knowing where to
go...
I think to myself I'm all alone and
don't know where to go...
I run faster and move quicker and
yet I can not loose this shadow...
It reached out to grab me and take
me away...
I woke up in the morning with tears
running down my face and realized I
was running from my own shadow.

Walking up the stairs, I felt warm
and calm inside…
I look up to the sky wondering
what's beyond the clouds…
I hear a voice calling me, telling me
to keep moving forward…
I see some friends along the way that
I hadn't seen in years…
They were all smiling and happy…
Just as I made it to the top of the
stairs, I woke up in bed and realized
I almost went to Heaven.

A friend never lets you down and is always there when you need them no matter what...
They listen and understand when you have a problem...
A friend will always encourage you when you have a dream or goal in mind...
They never make fun of you when you strike out or happen to be down on your luck...
A friend will always be honest with you, even if the truth hurts...
If we all had a best friend the world would be a happier place.

Man's best friend is always around
when you need him…
He's always loyal no matter what
you look like or how much money
you have…
He waits all day for your return and
when he sees you his tail wags from
side to side…
He'll sit with you all day and watch
all the games…
All he wants is love and loyalty in
return.

Heaven may not be white clouds or
angels with wings...
We may not see rainbows and
unicorns...
Although it may not be what we
expect...
I know it's going to be a place full of
love and joy...
We will feel no sorrow or pain...
We shall see our loved ones in
Heaven...
It will be a beautiful day.

Forever by our side...
Relate to our problems...
Involved in our life...
Educate us when we need help...
Never lie or take from us...
Deal with our ups and downs...
Save us from mistakes.

Love your family and friends...
Interesting and fun...
Find happiness where ever you can...
Embrace it and make it what you can.

Are with us all the time...
Never leave us when we need them...
Give us love and comfort...
Everyone has a special angel...
Love us no matter what we do...
Save us from making mistakes.

Lead me, guide me along the way
dear Lord...
How great thou art in everything
you do...
Will there be peace in the valley for
me..?
As the sun fell from the sky and day
became night, he touched me with his
love and glory...
I saw the love and passion as they
followed him around, he asked
himself many times, why me Lord...?
I walked around the place where the
King and his family lie; I felt the
presence of a sweet, sweet spirit
watching my every move...
Remember where ever you may go
you'll never walk alone.

Happiness for everyone...
Enter the gates and feel the love...
Angels we all become...
Very real place that we all go to...
Everlasting happiness we all share...
Never will we be alone in Heaven.

Always show your family how much
they're loved...
From a kiss on the cheek or a loving
hug...
Never take them for granted or loose
their love...
A family is important in the life we
live...
Love each and every one as if there
was no tomorrow.

Some people walk around in hate...
They look for a chance to hurt
another without a reason in the
world...
All of them fear what they do not
know...
They harm the innocent and pick on
the old...
One day they'll be taught a lesson
and do that no more.

Smile as you walk down the street...
Say hello to people you see...
Be kind and friendly with the ones
you love...
We get one chance at life; don't
waste it holding a grudge.

She made us laugh…
She made us smile…
Although she is gone…
We will never forget…
Her beautiful smile…
As I write this poem for you…
I know that your grandma will
always love and miss you.

She was sent from Heaven as our
little princess…
Although we only had this gift for a
short time…
We shall cherish her for a lifetime…
Our heart's and mind's tell us to cry
but we should not fear…
For where she has gone is a better
place…
Even though her body is no longer
here…

Her spirit has just left from our world to the Lord's care.

She was a bundle of joy sent from Heaven...
Although she was taken from us far too soon...
Her beautiful face and angelic voice...
Will remain in our hearts until we see her again...
Even though it may feel like an eternity...
We can feel safe knowing she is with the Lord, laughing and playing once again.

Look to the sky and wonder what's above the clouds...
Could it just be the stars and sun, or something more...?
As I ponder where we came from...
I stop to see the beauty in this life of ours...
For no matter who created this beauty, we should enjoy it while we can.

Sweet angel from Heaven...
Is spoiled and loved by her mommy...
Makes her way slowly but surely...
Big doggy with a tender heart...
Admired by all who meet her.

She walks slowly through the house
feeling her way around...
She does it with ease even though she
is blind...
She's a big hearted puppy who's
loved by all...
She loves to be outside in the hot
California sun...
If you take her for a run, you'd
better be quick...
Her name is Simba and she's our
favorite pup.

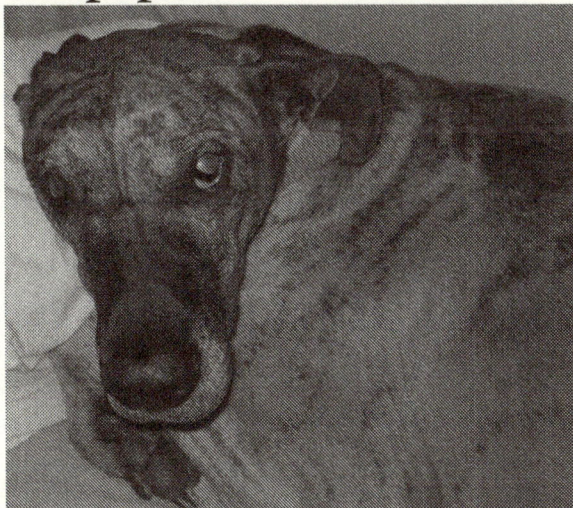

She was our sweet little angel that we loved and adored...
She was a caring and loving little pup that never harmed a soul...
She made us laugh and she made us cry...
She was taken from us before it was her time...
She went through the doggie door to Heaven and will be missed for all time.

Watching the clouds part in the big
blue sky...
I saw something moving just beyond
the clouds...
It had wings that were white and
full of long, thick feathers...
It soared in the sky ever so gently...
Standing there watching it go from
left to right...
I thought it was a bird that I'd
never seen before...
As it came closer I realized what it
was...
I saw a beautiful angel that came
down from Heaven and touched me
with its love.

Why do we waste time on things such as anger...
We should live our life as if there was no tomorrow...
We hurry through life without stopping to enjoy it...
The next time you see a rose, take the time to smell it.

Love can be all consuming if you let
it...
It can blind you in a second and
make you look like a fool...
If you learn how to love someone, it
can be the greatest gift that we're
given...
Just remember to control it, or it will
consume you too.

*We open our hearts to each other and
share our secrets…
We know that it's safe because our
hearts are one…
We finish each others sentences and
know what they're thinking…
We have an indescribable love that
we share with each other…
I think we're soul mates that met in
Heaven and now we get to show our
love on earth.*

Walking down the road I watch a
man and woman holding hands...
They watch out for each other and
keep close to one another...
Smiling and talking like a couple of
teenagers...
Fingers interlocked, hands holding
tight, they must have been together
for 50 years or so...
Still in love after that many years,
I've never seen a greater sight.

As we hurry about from day to day...
We should be reminded to slow down along the way...
Love and cherish every moment of your life...
For tomorrow could bring sadness and sorrow without any warning...
So remember to love one another and cherish everyday.

We may have worries and fears
about what lies ahead...
Enjoy life and make it the best that
you can...
Have fun and enjoy life and bring
joy to all that you can...
Take the time to count the stars and
enjoy them while you can...
Remember to help your brother along
the way, for the same God that made
you, made him too.

Do not fear death, for it's just
another part of life...
We may worry and wonder what we
will become...
We should not worry, for Heaven
awaits us...
I know there's something out there
bigger than you and me...
You'll know what it is, once you've
met me in Heaven.

After loving you, my heart felt
alive...
Because of love, I felt like a child in
a candy store...
Don't ask me why, but I love you
so...
You're my little earth angel and
you're always on my mind.

Watching the roses bloom in the
warm weather…
I'm reminded of how my mother
loved the roses…
She'd water them everyday and smell
each one as she made her way…
She smiled as they blossomed and
showed them to her friends…
Mama loved the roses that she
planted in the yard.

He is my everything, my Lord and savior…
Take my hand precious Lord, lead me home…
We call on him in our darkest hours…
If the Lord wasn't walking by my side, I wouldn't know where to go…
If we never meet again, thank you for all you've created.

Watching a man on the crowded city streets...
He stands there and asks people, could you spare any change...?
People pass him by and ignore him everyday...
He may not be dressed well or look very clean...
He's still a human being, just like you and me.

As I watch the kids run around the street...
I'm reminded of all the good times I had on the very same street...
We stayed outside for hours and played every game...
I no longer see the kids run around, or play games in the street...
What ever happened to the good old times when kids used their feet.

Walking along the ocean on a cold
and foggy night...
I feel someone is watching me but
there's no one in sight...
As I make my way along the foggy
shore...
I hear the voice of a man, singing
low and soft...
I couldn't make out the words
because of all the waves...
I like to think I know who it was
that sang on that very night.

Lifts your spirit…
Opens your mind to new things…
Vital part of our life…
Exciting and fun.

Help your fellow man…
Educate them whenever you can…
Appreciate everyone around…
Respect you friends and family…
Trust the people you love.

A love so pure and true is what we have together...
We know what the other is thinking without saying a word...
We show each other love from day to day...
We respect each other and share our dreams...
Soon we'll be man and wife and exchange rings that day.

As day becomes night I watch the
sun slowly fade away…
Walking down the street, I see some
lonely people walking by
themselves…
They seem to have no one and no
where to go…
They're completely lost souls not
knowing where to go.

We fall in love and give our heart to
one another...
We do all we can to show them how
much they're loved...
They return the love as fast as it's
received...
We pledge our ever lasting loyalty
with a band that's called a ring...
On this day that we exchange our
rings...
Two people become one, as they take
their first steps.

Krista

She is as beautiful as the bluest
waters of Hawaii...
As sweet as peach cobbler pie...
Her smile can light up the darkest of
sky's...
Although I now have her and know
she is mine...
I will never take her for granted this
love in my life.

Every time I hear a new born baby cry, I know the Lord has created another miracle...
Seeing their eyes open for the first time is a slice of Heaven on earth...
Their sweet and innocent inside, an angel of life...
We love and cherish them and thank God he gave them life.

The innocence of a child is the purest
thing in life...
You can see the innocence in their
eyes and smile...
Watch them as they look to the sky
and see a plane fly...
They know no prejudice and love
everyone they see...
The innocence of a child is the
sweetest thing.

As I watched the rain fall gently
from the sky...
I couldn't help but wonder, why
would God be crying...?
As I stood there in the rain, with all
the lightning and thunder...
I felt the sadness from his tears as
they fell from the Heavens...
The only thing I could tell him was,
it's ok to shed your tears.

As we mourn the passing of a dear
and loved one...
We should never feel alone, for
they're only just above us...
Although we cry and feel abandoned
because they're no longer with us...
We only need to remember, when our
time comes...
We'll be with them in Heaven, with
Jesus at our side, no longer feeling
the pain of all our lost loved ones.

Who created this world we live in...?
Could it be the man above...?
From the mountains to the oceans...
He's shown us his true love...
So help your brother along the way,
where ever you might be...
Remember that Jesus loves us, each
and everyone.

As day becomes night, the sky fills
up with twinkling lights...
I look outside my window,
wondering what they mean...
Each one telling a story of their
own...
As they send us love through their
beams of light...
I sit there and like to believe, it's our
loved ones in Heaven watching over
us as we sleep.

She stands there so sleek and sexy,
begging us to take a peek...
Her colors so bright and vibrant,
shining in the sun...
Wanting us to take her out and
show her to all who seek...
My mind starts to wonder as
memories fill my mind...
I remember all the good times and
long for the same once again...
I take her for a final spin, to all her
favorite spots...
I'll never forget the good times we
had, as I send her off to her final
resting spot.

*As I watched the rain fall gently to
the ground…
I wondered where it came from, as I
watched it leave the clouds…
I searched the sky and Heaven
above, with no answer to be
found…
As I stood there in the rain,
searching for an answer…
I looked up to the sky and the clouds
gently parted…
I felt the love of Jesus touch me and
the clouds went away.*

As I drive the city streets, I see all
the beauty along the way...
I stop to smell a rose and see it for
what it is...
A beautiful wonder of nature that
we sometimes need to stop and see...
It blossoms big and bright begging to
be noticed...
It seems to go unnoticed as people
pass it by...
The next time you're on the street,
take some time and enjoy a rose.

Sitting by myself on a dark and
lonesome road...
I drive down the highway not
knowing where to go...
I see a woman standing there
thumbing for a ride...
As I pull the car over and let her get
inside, she tells me she's been waiting
for me to give her a ride...
I ask her who she is and where she's
going...
She told me she was going to the
same place as I was...
Driving down the highway the signs
all read the same...
Next exit is Heaven, just one mile
away.

Circling the track in the black number
3...
He passes the challengers and does it
with ease...
He gave them that smile, as he pulled
up behind 'em...
He bumped 'em and rubbed 'em, to get
their attention...
Although he's in Heaven no longer
racing...
I sometimes still see him in the black
number 3.

He saved them and wrangled them to keep them safe...
They were protected and cared for, as he took them home...
His favorite word was Crikey!, it became a household phrase...
Steve Irwin saved them and showed us everyday.

As I sit here in my home writing
these poems...
I feel someone watching me yet there
is no one around...
I hesitate for a moment before I turn
to look...
It seems to want to tell me
something or let me know they are
always here...
I've never had this feeling before and
feel I know who it was.

I once felt a spirit shoot through my
soul...
It made me feel scared and
completely alone...
It was angry and tortured, an
unhappy soul...
Perhaps it's lonely and has no where
to go...
Now he's always with me and no
longer alone.

Elvis Through My Eyes

Driving around Memphis long after
midnight...
I realize that I'm driving with no
destination in mind...
I look to my right and who do I see,
Elvis Presley, the man, is sitting
next to me ...
I drive by a restaurant with its
lights burning bright...
Elvis tells me to pull in, so we can
grab a bite to eat...
Elvis was laughing and talking like
a child on Christmas Eve...
I drop him off by the gates of
Graceland and I bid him farewell...
I drive down the street to the Heart
Break Hotel...
I wake up the next morning and
what do I see, thousands of

mourners in line waiting to see the
King...
Tears started to flow slowly down
my face and I realized my time with
Elvis last night was only a dream.

A hundred years from now Elvis will
still be the King...
It's been thirty years now and he's
still the King of King's...
I know I won't be here 100 years
from now...
Which is why I spread the love for
him each and everyday.

As I sat there Crying In The
Chapel...
I couldn't help but wonder what had
happened...
Thoughts filled my mind and
emotions filled my heart...
Was Elvis really gone?
On the 30th anniversary of the
King's passing...
Say a special prayer for Elvis and his
family.

Elvis was a man who became a King...
I know he's with his family in Heaven, happy once again...
No matter how old I get Elvis, I'll Remember You.

Is It So Strange to admire a person so much?
I love him and never once have I met him...
He's a King among men and loved by millions...
His home attracts people from all over the planet...
He's out sold everyone around...
His name is Elvis Presley, don't ever forget it.

Seeing their faces with sorrow and
pain...
They lost the man they called the
King...
He was an everyday man who
became a legend...
He had thoughts and feelings like
you and me...
People expected him to be perfect in
everything he did...
Although he's gone and having fun
in Heaven, I'll have my chance to
meet him when God Calls Me Home.

I have a special piece of Memphis
that I carry in my heart...
It holds a special place in my mind
and I'll never let it go...
It has now become my Good Luck
Charm and will be for all time...
You'll never know what it is that I
carry in my heart.

I walked along his headstone with
tears in my eyes...
I look down and saw his name,
famous for all time...
I felt someone brush against me and
who did I see...
A man of six feet tall, who said his
name was Elvis Presley...
I stood there for a moment not
knowing what to say...

He said it's ok Mike, I'm no longer
in any pain...
I shook his hand not wanting to let
go, I was afraid his soul would pass
and I'd be all alone...
If we never meet again Mike, I'd
just like to say, I know what's in
your heart and I thank you everyday.

I listen to his music and look at his
picture...
I wonder if he's singing and
laughing once again...
They cried and fainted as the hearse
passed them by...
I'll Never Let You Go Elvis, a
woman cried with pain...
The King is gone and no longer with
us...

His fans still love him and will to the end.

I walk along the fresh cut grass...
I look over my shoulder and wonder
if he's watching me...
I follow the path he walked so many
years ago and think...
Am I really at the King's home..?
As I make my way along the curving
path...
I stop and wonder if his soul has
been set free...
I looked down to see the King lying
in his tomb...
Tears slowly fell from my face and I
realized the King is surely gone.

I know he wasn't perfect and made
mistakes along the way...
He was the shy boy from Tupelo,
Mississippi who was soon on his
way...
Although he was the King to
everyone around...
He was still a human being, with
feelings of his own deep down
inside...
Even with all of his friends and
entourage all around...
They never seemed to listen to most
of what he said...
He died of a broken heart, with
nobody around.

30th Anniversary

*Even though it's been thirty years
since that day...
We still long for the sound of your
voice and the smile that you gave...
We wait till that day when we can
tell you how much we loved you and
missed you everyday...
You brightened up our lives and gave
us love everyday...
We loved you so much Elvis, we all
had broken hearts that day.*

Pearly Gates

Although it's now been thirty years
since that sad day...
He's still the King of music no
matter what you say...
His fans will always love him and
remember the price that he paid...
He truly loved his fellow man and
wanted to help us everyday...
We still drive down to Graceland to
sit outside the gates...
We know where the King has gone
and that he made it to the pearly
gates.

As Elvis sat there recording his last
album...
Was he telling us the future without
giving us the answer...?
As he sang each song with such
sorrow and understanding...
He cried out for help and no one
responded...
Although he was the King to
everyone around...
He finally got their attention that
day the music died.

He sang of sorrow and loneliness on
his last album...
Did he know what was happening
and not want to tell us...?
He cried out for help, but we didn't
know what to do...
He feared he wouldn't be
remembered, he didn't know what to
do...
See that Elvis, all these years later
we remember you.

A lot of people said his music would never last...
I wish Elvis was here today to tell them "kiss my ass"...
Although they tried to change him and leave him in the past...
I wish Elvis was here today to kick them in the ass...
They may have never given him the credit he deserved...
I wish he was still here today to see the world he changed.

He was always around for his
friends and his family...
When he needed someone around, he
couldn't seem to find them...
He always took care of them and
gave them what they needed...
He was a kind and loving human
being with feelings of his own...
His friends seemed to leave him,
when he needed them the most...
Elvis died a lonely man, with no one
around.

July 5, 1954 saw a new era of music that would change the world...
He was a young boy from Memphis, Tennessee...
He sang with a style that had never been heard before...
He sang That's All Right Mama and the world has never been the same.

He lived life to the fullest...
Taking care of everyone around and
never asking for a thing back...
He spoiled everyone rotten and
always gave them more...
He had fun along the way and
changed the way we see things...
He's the King of music and will be
for all time.

He loved his fellow man and showed
us everyday...
He had a heart as big as the ocean...
He never asked a question and just
gave to those in need...
Giving almost all of what he had
and not knowing when to stop...
He always kept giving until his very
last days.

Elvis is still the King of music…
Played to sold out arenas…
Revolutionized music for all time…
Taking care of business in Heaven…
It has been different without him…
Final resting place, Graceland…
Imprisoned in his own home…
He evolved as an entertainer…
Is the greatest voice of all time…
He is a king among men.

Humble and caring person...
Over looked as a humanitarian...
Wonderful and loving soul...
Greatest singer of all time
Resting in peace with his family...
Elvis is in Heaven with his mom...
Amazing personality and smile...
Taught us how to have fun...
Tragically died far too young...
He always took care of business...
Opened his heart for us too see...
Unbelievable human being...
An amazing performer...
Rightfully remembered for all time...
Told us to love our fellow man.

Made us laugh all the time…
You inspired us with your voice…
Wished I could have met you…
An amazing soul, taken too soon…
You are remembered with love.

A beautiful smile and laugh…
My hero for all time
Educated us through his music…
Never gave up on life.

Dedicated his life to music...
On our minds everyday...
Never forget Elvis...
Tough yet loving to his friends...
Best performer we've ever seen...
Elvis, we miss you everyday...
Cool and calm, a true superstar...
Regarded as the best of all time...
Unbelievable voice and charm...
Elvis we love you...
Laying in peace at Graceland.

The world stood still that day the
King died...
We felt lost and confused when we
heard the news...
How could Elvis die? He wasn't
supposed to leave us so soon...
He had so much more to give and
teach us, I'm still a little confused...
How could he have left us, without
saying goodbye...?
We were broken hearted and blue the
day Elvis died...
We love you and miss you Elvis and
wish you were alive.

Forever in our hearts...
Everlasting fame and love...
Very important person to millions...
Elvis was the last great hero...
Remember the King.

Felt his soul at Graceland...
On our minds day to day...
Our fallen hero...
Loved and cared for everyone.

Inspired us everyday...
Joined his family in Heaven...
Opened his heart to the world...
Had a beautiful soul...
Never let him go.

I walked around Graceland not
knowing what to think...
I wondered if Elvis was watching
me from the sky so high above...
I felt something more as I stood by
his grave...
I couldn't help but cry and shed all
my tears...
As I stood there in front of the
King...
I told him I loved him and wished he
hadn't died.

He always came out to see us, when
we stood outside the music gates...
For some, meeting him seemed to be
the impossible dream...
No matter who you were or what
you looked like...
Elvis talked to everyone and signed
everything that was handed on
down...
So as you go to Graceland and stand
outside the gates, just remember the
King's inside resting, in his final
place.

Elvis believed in wearing both a Cross and Chai symbol to make sure he didn't miss out on Heaven.

Walking in the dark on a quiet and
lonely street...
I think to myself, I'm in Memphis,
not far from the King...
As I walk slowly down the street, I
hear someone's foot steps slowly
following me...
Making my way towards Graceland,
I wonder what I'll see...
Looking over the wall to see the
home of the King...
I see the shadow of a man, about six
feet tall...
As he makes his way to the King's
resting place...
He looks my way as he smiles and
throws me a wave...
Before I know it, the man is gone, I
could be crazy but I saw his shadow
jump into his grave.

Standing by the gates of Graceland I
wait for the man…
Watching the front door to get a
glimpse of the King…
As I stand there for hours with no
sign of his face…
I yell out, hey Elvis, how much
longer are you gonna make me
wait…?
As I waited all night, standing on
my feet…
A stranger walks by and stops for a
second…
She's asks me what I'm doing and
who I'm waiting for…
I tell her who else lady, but the King
of King's…
As I stand there waiting to see
Elvis, she slowly starts to tell me,
sorry son but the King is dead.

As I drove down the street, I couldn't help but stop and turn around...
Following her down the street I tried my hardest to keep up...
She started moving faster, as I tried to catch up...
I stepped on the gas and gave it all I had...
I pulled up alongside this beautiful car and saw who was driving...
Once I realized who it was, his Cadillac stepped on the gas and left me in the dust.

I pulled up to a diner on a lonesome
and dark road…
Parking next to a Cadillac that I had
seen once before…
I stepped inside the restaurant and
looked all around…
Seeing a man at the counter sitting
by himself…
I sat next to him and introduced
myself…
He said how ya doin son? Sorry
about leaving ya in the dust…
As I sat there and talked, I knew
who he was…
I paid for his dinner and he told me
goodbye…
I'll see ya around Elvis, I hope
you're living a good life.

He truly believed in building the
kingdom of Heaven on earth...
The Lord knows he wasn't perfect
but did the best he could under the
circumstances...
He tried his best to never let us
down...
Some people took him for granted
and lost sight of who he was...
He wanted us all to have the best
things in life...
He made mistakes along the way,
just like you and me...
Which is what made him a normal
human being...
His "friends" still cling to his name,
to grab a piece of the spotlight...
Some of them say how bad of a
human being he was...

Although he took care of them and
gave them all they needed...
They still run his name through the
mud and seem to have no shame...
To those who feel the need to make
him look bad...
Name something that you've done, to
help your fellow man!

I saw a blue light in Memphis...
That spoke to me with its soul...
Begging to be noticed, as it made its
presence known...
Its spirit shot right through me, like
a bullet from its barrel...
It made me shake and tremble, as I
almost fell to the floor...
Was this blue image in my picture
Elvis, or perhaps some other lost
soul?

Never had I seen something so
unhappy and sad...
It looked right at me, as if it were
alive...
It made me tremble with fear and
almost made me cry...
It seemed to have taken a part of my
soul to some other place I had never
been before...
I don't know who it is or why it
chose me, I just wish I hadn't seen it
in Memphis, Tennessee.

I titled this book, Through My Eyes for a specific reason. Elvis had always wanted to write a book with that title. Unfortunately he never had the chance; I can only imagine how wonderful a book it would have been. I hope this book is close to what he had in mind. He loved life and everything about it. I truly hope where ever he may be, he's happy and knows how much he was and is loved to this day.

You have seen things through my eyes and know how I feel. I have also tried to see things through Elvis' eyes and wonder how he felt. I know he believed in seeing visions and being able to heal people, which in my opinion, is a beautiful thought. He should be remembered for the compassionate and caring person that he was.

He had something special that we can't quite figure out or put our finger on. Elvis was more than a man and less than a God, which is why he's the King. I truly believe he was given a special gift and was meant to share it with the world.

We go through life searching for answers to questions we feel need to be answered. I myself have wondered where we came from and why we're here. I wish I had the answer every one is looking for, but I don't. I never thought there was something else out there until I had my experience just after visiting Graceland. Since that day, I have felt a different connection to Elvis and know something more lies ahead.

Now, I search for an answer as to why we're here and what our purpose is. I don't think anyone should use every minute of their life searching for an answer. Enjoy life while you're here but stop to take the time to question things along the way. Some people waste a lifetime searching for an answer and never find what they're looking for. The answers appear when you least expect it.

The Human Side of Elvis

People sometimes forget that even Elvis was a human being with feelings and emotions of his own. He had given so much of himself to his fans, friends and family that some people forgot to ask how he was doing. Towards the end of his life he had physical problems that affected his outward appearance. People started to make fun and say mean and disrespectful things about him. Everyone seemed to forget that he was still the caring and generous person he had always been, but he was being judged based on looks even after all the wonderful things he had done to help people. Always try to remember we only get one chance at life and we should make the best of it. We all change as we get older but we should never treat someone mean or with disrespect because they change on the outside. I myself will always admire Elvis for being the person he was and for being able to survive for as long as he did with the pressure he was under. I can only hope he knows how much he has affected people in so many wonderful ways. For one man to inspire and attract so many people even 30 years after his death, I think it's easy to say he had something special deep within his soul. I wish he were alive today to see how he has affected people in so many positive ways.

I feel lucky to have been touched by his love and soul. If it weren't for

Elvis being who he was and loving people the way he did, I wouldn't be the person I am today.

It's very hard to make a non Elvis fan understand who he was. I guess it's because they haven't been touched by his love and soul. It's a special feeling that I guess not everyone gets to experience.

Remember, it doesn't matter what you're passionate about, just as long as you have passion. Never let anyone tell you what you care about doesn't matter.

Elvis' philosophy for a happy life

SOMEONE TO LOVE,
SOMETHING TO LOOK
FORWARD TO, AND
SOMETHING TO DO!

E.P. 1972

Although it may be a short and simple philosophy, it's perfect. We all need someone to love no matter who we are. Having something to look forward to is important in life and keeps us motivated. Having something to do, keeps us on our toes and reminds us that were still alive.

I hope you have enjoyed seeing things Through My Eyes. We all see different things in life which is why I wanted to share. Just remember that everyone has feelings deep down inside and we should try to treat them with love and respect.

www.ingramcontent.com/pod-product-compliance
Lightning Source LLC
Chambersburg PA
CBHW030520100426
42813CB00001B/96